The Voice Unheard

Anvita Mathur

BookLeaf Publishing

India | USA | UK

Made with ❤ on the BookLeaf Publishing Platform
www.bookleafpub.in
www.bookleafpub.com

Dedication

I would like to dedicate this book firstly to both my grandfathers. My nana Dr S.S Mathur (*Madhukar)* from whom I've inherited my writing skills and love for poems, and my baba Late Mr B.N Mathur whose absence and memories nudged me to let my emotions out.

I'll always be grateful to my mother, Mrs. Kavita Mathur, who is my pillar of strength, whose unwavering support has always fueled my dreams. My father, Mr Bhuvenesh Mathur, from whom I learnt to be brave enough to speak my mind. And my grandmothers Mrs Pushpa Mathur and Mrs Sudha Mathur, two strong women of very different kind, from whose words and actions I've learnt a lot. Most importantly to my little sister Miss Tanisha Mathur, my heart in human form, the light that brightens my life. And to my two best friends Mrs Aparajita and Mr Nimesh Vijayvargiya, who always stand by me through every season of life.

This book is a piece of my soul, and a tribute to the love, life and experiences that shaped it.

Preface

These poems are an expression of the thoughts I've held in my heart for years. They are deeply personal to me. This is the first time I've ever expressed myself so openly. This isn't a commercial or professional attempt but simply a girl trying to express herself.

Every word in this book comes straight from the heart, reflecting the emotions I've seen, felt, and lived through so far. Love, loss, joy, confusion, hope—they all find their place in these pages.

This collection doesn't follow a strict structure or narrative. Instead, it flows like emotions, unpredictable yet intimate. Some pieces might feel relatable, while others offer a small glimpse of my world.

Thank you to everyone who gave me the courage and opportunity to pour my heart out. I hope my words resonate with you, even in the smallest of ways.

Acknowledgements

This book would not have been possible without the love
and support and encouragement of my mother, who is
my constant source of confidence and inspiration. I
would like to thank my family their constant support
and thoughts and from whose life I could draw
inspiration for each of my poems. To my friends for
listening to me always, and for taking care of me and
accepting everything about me. Special thanks to my
little sister- My source of strength who everyday proves
to me that vulnerability is not a weakness.
To my aunts and uncles, cousins and everyone who has
inspired a line, a thought, or a feeling in this book,
whether you know it or not, thank you.
And most of all I'm thankful to the readers holding this
book for giving me chance to share my thoughts and
voice with you.

1. THE VOICE UNHEARD

This is my voice unheard,
sharing these with all is a bit awkward.

All these years, I hid it away,
kept this part of me at bay.

This courage was too hard to find,
to express openly what's on my mind.

I'm the less expressive introverted soul,
but once in lifetime being heard was the goal.

I can't convey it in so many words directly,
only through my poems I can express correctly.

This is my voice unheard,
sharing these with all is a bit awkward.

Lone wolf might be my spirit animal, headstrong,
but sometimes I need to be understood and belong.

Good listener with high empathy,
with great advises, evidently.

Now I want my container to crack,
want to belong and open up to my pack.

I'm taking this chance to let my voice be heard,
wish to prove myself, my fear of being see, absurd.

This is my voice unheard,
some might even love it, now it occurred.

2. WHY HESITATE TO COMMUNICATE

Why are we so scared to communicate,
Are we afraid it'll open the flood gate.

But wouldn't it grow our internal sense of hate,
Shouldn't we let it out before it's too late.

Are we too scared to explore our fate,
And trying to freeze our current state.

I've never seen anyone express themselves truly, till date,
Are we all trying to struggle lone behind the closed gate.

If only we could be more honest at least with our mate,
Wouldn't it make relationships easier and life great.

When will we all understand the importance to
communicate,
That's the day the people of the world truly await.

We need to express our feelings straight,
They'll understand themselves; we need to avoid that
wait.

The hurt of not being understood carries lot of weight,
But sometimes that is hard for other to estimate.

Then we tend to have all these moments in our heart collate,
Which brings our relationship downstate.

'Drop the hint' on which we fixate,
That might be hurting them too, we don't evaluate.

When we form a new relationship, thinking alike isn't a mandate,
Then why to misalignment we retaliate.

Why are we so scared to communicate,
Just try to express yourself and let that bubble in your heart deflate.

3. PHOENIX ON RISE

Girl, it's time to wipe tear from your lashes,
And rise above like phoenix from its ashes.

Now is the time to reap what you sowed,
That's enough time life has made you bowed.

Life tends to test the most its finest warriors,
You have burned in agony for years.

You don't know how strong you are,
The world will acknowledge it, the day is not far.

The most blazing star are the ones that shine brightest,
Don't self-doubt even the slightest.

Your guardian angels are smiling down on you,
They paved your way even before you knew.

Girl it's time to wipe tear from your lashes,
And rise above like phoenix from its ashes.

All these years you faced the storms with all your might,
Endured all the moments tongue tied.

Listen to what your guts are screaming,
You have the most powerful intuitive feeling.

Just when the life is about to reward your endurance,
Just don't lose your patience.

You don't know how much you've made your loved ones proud,
Even the ones who criticize will come around.

This might be your hardest test of perseverance,
The last challenge is self-acceptance.

Girl it's time to wipe tear from your lashes,
And rise above like phoenix from its ashes.

4. LETTER TO GRANDFATHER

I know we would a lot disagree,
But our aligned output was quite gutsy.

You left without even proper goodbye,
That was mean of you to make us all cry.

I know I don't express myself so well,
But we still needed time to bid you farewell.

They say my strength and anger sometimes resemble
yours,
So, I'll be able to provide them with that strength, that
reassures.

Your presence still marks every corner and situation,
Things you disliked, in my heart still cause agitation.

I still sometime hear your voices in my head,
And your visit in my dreams seems godsent.

I know you're watching us from afar,
I assure I won't allow our family to drop the bar.

I know you hated us being weak,
Your boldness and strength are all we seek.

I know I don't express myself well,
But we still needed time to bid you farewell.

We're all out there trying to achieve what you dreamed,
I assure you; you would've been relieved.

There still might be things that you may have not
approved,
But still some that would've had you moved.

I know you liked even how we fought,
Holding my ground is what you've taught.

I remember how you shared your mind with me,
Made me your messenger and watching from above in
all glee.

Sometimes I try to contribute your part in family,
So that they can just remember you happily.

I know I don't express myself so well,
But we still needed time to bid you farewell.

5. LOYALTY

Loyalty these days is so underrated,
The world, our historic heroes would've truly hated.

They fought all wars so honorably,
Now we're picking our battles grayly.

Disloyal men have history and mythology truly
condemn,
They were the ones who cause worst mayhem.

Today our everyday battles aren't as severe,
Then why are our loyalties still unclear.

Why do we accept relations carrying distrust,
Isn't fidelity a must.

Are those small wins of that importance?
More than losing loved one's confidence.

Loyalty these days is so underrated,
Our trust is being traded.

Even the bravest solider needs loyal team,
To protect themselves from opponent's scheme.

Even the nature keeps setting the example,
The dogs and horses are some examples.

Real friend is the one you can trust blindly,
They're the real gems, so choose wisely.

Loyalty should be looked up to highly,
People aren't understanding this, sadly.

Loyalty these days is so underrated,
Maybe our good days are dated.

6. LETTER TO YOUNG ME

Hey little one, are you doing fine?
You know, you're worth every dime.

Don't worry you'll age like a fine wine,
You're a piece of work so divine.

Don't be scared and stay confine,
You can achieve anything that you determine.

Everyday comes with a new sunshine,
There are skills at which you outshine.

I know this teenage feel like field of landmine,
But know this, that all your efforts to success are inline.

There is no life formula or guideline,
You'll even question your worth sometime.

Just find your center and internal shrine,
That'll guide you to your path everytime.

Don't always bend away, just have a strong spine,
You'll value your strong sense of value and ethics in your
prime.

What your trophy is, you'll have to define,
No one should give you your life's outline.

You're the main character in your story, don't stand on sideline,
You'll have to play on frontline.

No, you don't need the smallest waistline,
Nor do you need to be the next Einstein.

Life has too many unique experiences for you in pipeline,
So, pounce on it like the strongest canine.

7. BABY SISTER

I hate how much love for my sister I carry,
How protective I'm of her is quite scary.

She makes me mad all the time,
But her stupid innocent smile, makes it all fine.

What is she always up to, leaves me curious,
Her carefree attitude leaves me furious.

If I could, I would install camera to her head,
And sleep peacefully on my bed.

She gives us scares that have us always worried,
How much I worry, I have to keep it buried.

She makes me feel old already,
And nagging her always makes me feel petty.

I hate how much love for my sister I carry,
How protective I'm of her is quite scary.

I still see her as a little baby,
Overthinking much, definitely maybe.

I know she thinks I'm the worst of her guardian,
Maybe even as the angry demon.

I don't care as long as I can watch over her,
Life before looking out for her is quite blur.

I don't know how to turn this off,
Even if my smothering makes her cough.

Maybe someday my feelings she'll understand,
And see things clearly with that thickhead.

8. RACE OF LIFE

What are we running after,
Is it money or heart full of laughter.

Why we spend more days worrying and whining,
Even when the beautiful sun on head is shining.

Maybe this sense of needing more, just greed,
Maybe the real satisfaction is in doing the good deed.

Maybe we should be on ourselves a little less hard,
And not build our life like house of card.

Maybe we need to live the journey more,
Who knows how much lifeline we bore.

Life is not on the other side of finish line,
But to live through this limited track of time.

Life gives us so many unique moments to live by,
In the constant seek for better future, we let it fly by.

We're sprinting through life like a 100-meter race,
It's a long marathon, so hold your pace.

There is no definition of perfect life,
Joy in little things only keeps us alive.

Have it all and still feel dissatisfaction,
Or live life to fullest, even in fraction.

What are we running after,
The finish line or the journey full of laughter.

9. THE IDEAL COMPANION

Who is an ideal companion?
Someone enlighten me or I go sit under baniyan?

How am I to choose the one,
The one who'll add to or take away the fun.

Is the one who would take my responsibility until my
last day,
Or the one who would hold my back and push me
through my paved way?

I had dreams of perfect man of my own,
Who would acceptingly measure the heights I've flown.

I believed my companion would be to whom I can bare,
What I feel and need, he would care.

They tell me I'm too picky for my own good,
But I've lived by the book to earn the partner who
understood.

Who is an ideal companion?
Someone enlighten me or I go sit under baniyan?

Should he be fair, handsome, and tall?
Or someone who'll catch me when I fall?

Maybe I want all this and more,
The one whose presence make me twirl around on floor.

A girl is supposed to live her own fairytale,
What's mine is soon to unveil.

I wonder what will make me choose my man,
What would make me commit to a situation from which
I always ran.

I just wish he can understand my words unsaid,
I wonder who's on the other end of my red thread.

10. TANGLED EXPECTATION

They tell me to find myself a man,
Sounds like they already have a plan.

Almost 30 years of my life I learned to live
independently,
Now they want me to act a damsel vehemently.

Pre-teen, teen, adulthood all I lived restrained,
How am I now supposed to open my heart, I wasn't
trained.

The "marriageable age" has my beliefs shaken,
Suddenly all people care for me is to be "taken".

One who is handsome, caring, and smart, why can't I
expect to have all of it?
The one who checks all boxes and is the right fit.

Isn't the society half made of women with dreams like
me?
All trying to find their prince out of Disney.

Are we losing the focus from the real idea of
companionship?
Wasn't marriage all about finding ideal partnership, not
kinship.

You didn't like anyone yet, they ask,
They do seem to all wear a hypocritical mask.

For first 25 years of my life, I was told it's a bad idea to
date,
All I could care about was getting good grade.

Now they ask me if I have anyone on mind,
Please tell them I don't know where to find.

After 27 they ask me to already marry,
I couldn't even process the hurry.

Can someone teach me how to fall for a guy,
I don't know how to talk like that, can't deny.

I think I wasn't taught to initiate the courtship,
I think the right one will have to lead this relationship.

11. THE QUEEN

Once there was a daddy's little princess, a beauty,
So pure and sweet, far away from life worldly.

Then she grew up into a finest maiden,
Married a man that her parents chosen.

Her life turned upside down,
Little princess now had to bear the weight of queen
crown.

Soon a mother, her responsibilities only grew,
She faced bravely all the curveballs life threw.

She started to live her dreams through her two
princesses,
She smiled and laughed for them, even during distresses.

To give them everything they ever wished for and more,
In her work and care, her heart she poured.

Never complained about all she had to endure to protect
them from all,
Her needs and expectations from life grew small.

Queen to the world, at home was just a perfect wife,
mother, and daughter-in-law,
Too afraid to let anyone point out in her work any flaw.

A nurse to ailing, cook in kitchen and doing laundry,
Loving and nurturing her family became her story.

Then grew up her daughters who stepped out of their
cocoon,
Realizing having such strong and sacrificing mother was
such a boon.

She gave her beauty and wings to her little princesses,
How grateful they are, the words can't express.

Through this all, daddy's little princess lost her prime
time,
If she had more time for herself and didn't live confine.

Her talents and dreams, she locked them away,
Sincere gratitude, her family should convey.

Once there was a daddy's little princess, a beauty,
To take care of her health and happiness is now our duty.

12. SEASONS OF SOUL

Winter makes me cherish the warmth and just stay,
Beautiful view and warm drink all day.
O my heart, it feels so cozy,
Gives a cold blush, so rosy.

Autumn brings the shades of orange,
The way I feel the roller-coaster of emotions is quite
strange.
Carpet of leaves nudge me to find new path,
Feels like I'm walking into finest art.

Rain washes away the pain,
Cry it all out and make room for new gain.
Reminds me to hold my own umbrella,
I am no damsel nor Cinderella.

Summer brings out sun so bright,
Negative thoughts, I'm ready to fight.
Let yourself lose in summer breeze,
There's so much for you to seize.

The spring brings the joy so sweet,
The glee it brings nothing can beat.
Seeing all flowers at their full blossom,
Remind myself that life is awesome.

13. THE MAN OF OUR HOUSE

The man whose life revolves around friends and family,
Just needs sweets and chai daily.

Shouldered responsibilities so young to help his father,
Grew with naughty kid image, he was much kind and smarter.

Growing older he faced so many hard days,
Made him stronger that even worst couldn't have him fazed.

Loved his two little sisters like children of his own,
For them he would give up any throne.

A dotting son to mother he loved more than his life,
If she asked him to, the whole world he would sacrifice.

Cool dad to his little daughters who shared his humor and wit,
When he set his heart to, they never saw him quit.

There's no responsibility he didn't fulfill,
Still, he carries a demeanor so chill.

For him, his friends are as important as his family,
He'll do anything for them happily.

His wife is his constant source of strength,
Who gets him without words and understands his intents.

He's a workaholic whose favorite time is in office,
Still any family event, he would never miss.

He's the man one will find beside them in their hard days,
He tries to help them all in his own ways.

An honest officer, makes all proud,
He did what he found ethical and right throughout.

Refusing to accept his old age, he swifts through like a powerhouse,
That is the man of our house.

14. THREE MESSY PIECES, WE BESTIES

We three messy pieces but together a masterpiece,
Like air, water, fire, we have different personalities.

One is like fire protecting with his constant warmth all
around,
Try to hurt us and his wrath will burn you to ground.
Heart of passion and pillar of strength,
For us he'll go to any length.

Then comes the air, cool breeze fostering the sensibility,
Anger her once and you'll regret instantly.
Rustling through life and whispering wise words,
Just her presence always comforts.

Then I flow into their lives like water emotionally,
They manage my storms happily.
Transparent but with a lot of depth,
Calmest of all but stormy when wept.

These three elements might make steam sometime,
But balances each other like perfect partner in crime.

When air and water are causing cyclone uncontrolled,
Fire is saving others from harsh cold.

When fire and water cause the steam,
Air tries to dissipate it with cool breeze.

When air and fire are causing explosion,
Water is willing to absorb the implosion.

We three messy pieces but together a masterpiece,
Like air, water, fire we bestie bring each other peace.

15. POWER OF KINDNESS

Wish we lived in world so kind,
We could leave all grief behind.

A little gesture can make someone's day,
A huge impact you can have with the kind words you
say.

In this fast world there are so many lost and lonely souls,
Living with heavy heart full of holes.

If we bring this change collectively,
It'll heal the whole community well-being.

Bring a little smile to someone's face,
astonishing number of blessings you'll embrace.

They say kindness has ripple effect of positivity,
Increases the social sensitivity.

Maybe this will reinstate the world's faith in goodness,
To cure this hatred and negativity illness.

Wish we lived in world so kind,
We could leave all grief behind.

Funny how being kind to others can heal our own heart,
Also fill up our karmic cart.

Kind heart doesn't get affected easily,
They even give it all up for others gleefully.

They know that karma and heaven above is looking over,
Their justice is strong even if slower.

Power of kindness is so underrated,
There is no kindness that goes wasted.

They'll forever remember the kind one they met,
They debt of kindness they'll forever try to offset.

Wish we lived in world so kind,
We could leave all grief behind.

16. TWO BRANCHES OF THE SAME TREE

We are two branches of the same tree,
But with opposite personality.

She's a little tweety bird, sweet and chirpy,
I'm more protective canine, looking out for my birdy.

She is so full of ideas so crazy,
Though I have to admit, the ideas are quite brainy.

On the other hand, I live very carefully,
I guess our parents needed at least one to live sincerely.

One is night owl other morning daisy,
Raising us must've not been easy.

Though we have choices completely opposite,
Still, it is so hard to keep her out of my closet.

She loses her stuff so quickly,
While I need my stuff in place strictly.

We are two branches of the same tree,
But with opposite personality.

We're different type but with common roots,
Our parent's nightmare when in cahoots.

She is sun and me the moon,
To our differences we're quite immune.

Her optimism and my reliability,
Open doors to a lot of possibilities.

She's practical and I'm dreamy,
Together we complete this family.

We are two branches of the same tree,
But with opposite personality.

17. FLOWER HEART

I seem to have the heart of flower,
Different kinds give it power.

Innocent and pure as lily,
One that wakes up with good intentions daily.

Graceful and gentle like rose,
Give my personality gentleness dose.

Fresh and bright as daisy,
Never let me feel lazy.

Royalty and elegance of orchid,
Never lets my value drip.

Bright and loyal like sunflower,
Let me hold their back even in darkest hour.

Wise and full of hope like iris,
Let my heart remain deeply pious.

Empathetic and understanding like hydrangea,
Allow me to help them release their fear.

Strong sense of lasting affection like zinnia,
Help keep my heart warm with the love 'diya'.

Youth and joy of lilac,
Always keep me young and wouldn't let my dreams lack.

The warmth and creativity of marigold,
Gives me strength to make decisions so bold.

Enlightenment of the lotus,
Reminds me to keep my focus.

Dignity of dahlia,
Doesn't let me entertain unethical idea.

Nostalgia of forget-me-not,
Keeps reminding me of all the lessons life taught.

Serenity and calmness of lavender,
Doesn't let my heart and desires wander.

I seem to have heart of flower,
Different kinds give it power.

18. THE NEW ME IN NEW WORLD

When I stepped out into new world to explore,
In the new country of Singapore.

Met new friends who became family,
They embraced me in, so warmly.

Our friendship bridged the culture and language gap,
A beautiful journey unwrapped.

Learning about different beliefs left me in awe,
Experienced so many things that I never saw.

From Filipino friendliness to Chinese hospitality, I loved
it all so much,
But most importantly how they made me feel special, I
was touched.

Inclusiveness of Singaporeans and empowering
Indonesians, my deep respect,
I got more comfortable, than I could expect.

Japanese and Thai were so supportive,
While Europeans were so positive.

In return I could share about my culture with delight,
And they made sure I felt appreciated and heard with
excite.

I can't be more grateful for their friendship and
politeness,
No matter I'll never lose these friendships, priceless.

I loved Singapore not just because it is a beautiful first
world country,
But how all the cultures and races co-exist so
respectfully.

They accepted me like one of their own so graciously,
Took care of me like a family.

They made me discover a side of myself so new,
And made me see the world with a different view.

When I stepped out into new world to explore,
I gained new experience and relationship that I never
had before.

19. FRIENDS

True friends are for life,
Faces that always make you smile.

They maybe far away,
But friendship is going to stay.
They've not just seen you grow,
But also, your highs and lows.
They don't need flatter,
They'll hold your back no matter.

Our love for each other is so unique,
We feel it even when we don't speak.
I miss all those good old days,
Without friends, I'll feel astray.
I was never the one to act silly,
But with them I can be one daily.
I've learnt so much from them,
That's where grew my crazy stem.

Friends are for life,
Without them, don't know how to survive.

20. PARENTS, THE SUPERHUMAN?

Are our parents humans just like us?
Who also once made similar fuss?

Weren't they supposed to be superhumans that made no
mistakes,
Or were they forced to be more careful, for our sake.

Do they also sometime wish to break free and run wild,
Or were they just born so refined?

Why is it so hard to see them more human with flaws?
For their efforts deserve an applause.

But I think that hero image we built for them is unfair,
Because we cannot accept them making mistakes
anywhere.

Maybe if we saw them as normal people like us,
And before judging and reacting, we discuss.

As we're all growing older,
And starting to have similar expectations on our
shoulder.

This revelation is harder to accept,
they could be wrong too, I'm stressed.

Who will now take all the responsibility,
I don't think I have their superhuman ability.

Their aging hands make them more human every day,
How we'll ever accept this, can't say.

21. THE JOB DESPAIR

No job is a scare,
But unfulfilling job cause despair.

The job break is scare,
No hearing call back cause despair.

Not doing well at job is a scare,
Not having time to upgrade ourselves cause despair.

Retrenchment period is a scare,
Being called out as under or overqualified after hardwork
cause despair.

Job hunting period brings out under confidence and
scare,
But then never having an off period to explore ourselves
cause despair.

Is it being so hard on ourselves any fair?
Neglecting that our life has so many layer.

Maybe the gap is to be filled with other flair,
To find our true self and our talents, we dare.

We work to live not live to work, I swear,
Find true happiness and content is what we need to care.

Finding positive in such times is rare,
But maybe it was an answer to our prayer.

Life tests us in so many ways, don't know when and
where,
But all our life journeys are unique, can't compare.

We're all struggling mentally and seeking help with
joined pair,
God has better plan, but we criticize life unaware.

Professional break might look like a big scare,
But this time might bring you better opportunities and
save you from despair.

22. IDEAL DAUGHTER

Who is an 'ideal daughter'?
Is it the one who they let society slaughter.

Be respectful and nice to everyone no matter they say,
But when will that ever repay?

No romance and don't date,
Then when she doesn't marry, they hate.

Go excel professionally and make us proud,
But what to do when all try to bring her down.

Dress modestly and have humility,
Then compare her looks to celebrity.

Don't talk back for family harmony,
Then ask her why she avoid all company.

Taught her to love all and care,
But taking decisions for them, she can't dare.

Do all the work to perfection,
Then why there is still no sense of satisfaction?

Oldest daughter and granddaughter title come with
greatest responsibilities,
Making her question everyday her capabilities.

Be elegant and dress to show our nobility,
But all this makes her retract her sociability.

It's so hard to carry two personalities,
Honestly can't tell who is more she.

Where is her 'ideal daughter' crown?
whose life has been all about preventing that frown.

23. LIFE JOURNEY

There's more to life than his smile.
He wasn't worth even a single second of your time.

Life is a journey pretty long.
You need to be more careful to what you need to hold
on.

People come and people go.
Only the right ones will see you through it all.

Some people come just to hurt and make you feel small.
But only to teach you how to be more strong.

Life is a journey too long,
if you can't forgive them all.

There is a teaching in every wrong,
Learn and accept it and move on.

Someday someone will hold your hand.
Why all didn't work out, you'll understand.

All the bad memories aren't made to remind you of your
mistakes,
But to remind, you have what it takes.

Don't feel that you've lost your way.
start afresh, it's a new day.

Forgive the people who hurt you bad.
They showed you what you had.

Life is a journey too long.
Brace yourself up and move along.

24. THE NIGHT

My favorite time of the day,
The quiet of night when they all hit the hay.

When the moonlit sky looks O' so serene,
View prettier than my dream.
The quiet of the night lets my inner voice be loud,
The feeling of calmness is profound.
The sweet fragrance of flowers is intoxicating,
Like all the night angels are out celebrating.
Sad or happy the night reflects my mood,
For my empty heart it becomes a soul food.
The bright stars in sky glimmers,
In my eyes the hope shimmers.
On the nights I feel hopeless and dazed,
The dark velvety sky envelops me into comfortable
embrace.

My favorite time of the day,
The quiet of night when they all hit the hay.

I own my time at night like a queen bee,
Which daytime always steal away from me.
I can do whatever that my heart desire,
I don't have to go around to put out fire.

I can enjoy my love for music and writing,
Or just enjoy the peace of night while reading.
My favorite time of the day,
The night when from life I run away.

25. GRATITUDE TO LIFE

To life I feel deep gratitude,
It gave me more despite that grumbling attitude.

To younger me who felt life unfair,
how blessed your life is, be aware.

The moments of power and money will take you only so
far,
It's your caring heart and pure soul that'll define who
you are.

We all see both good and bad days,
Good are blessings while bad show you better ways.

To life I feel deep gratitude,
It gave me more despite that grumbling attitude.

Most life I kept myself shell locked,
Scared of being judged and mocked.

Why care for what they think as long as I'm on path of
betterment,
Real riches of life are love and contentment.

I have enough to fulfill my needs, wants and more,
But real happiness came from sharing with indigent at
my door.

Most my relations bring me love and joy,
Who wants more when I have people I love and time to
enjoy.

There are still times when I forget to count my blessings,
I'm still growing, I'm fessing.

26. IF I COULD READ MIND...

If I could read mind,
Know true intentions they hide.

Maybe I would know who to trust,
And who's niceness was a complete bust.

Some may sound harsh but mean well,
While some sweeter talkers create false spell.

If I could read mind,
I could weed out those who leave humanity maligned.

'Oh, you're doing so well' they cast an evil eye,
Then put you through situations that make you cry.

While others with the harshest words of advice,
If you could take it, they're your true allies.

Not all those sweet ones are wearing a disguise,
But who is genuine, it's important to recognize.

If I could read mind,
The true ones wouldn't have been so hard to find.

I once trusted ones who found pleasure in my misery,
What they gained out of it is still a mystery.

They broke my trust time and again,
I locked my heart up with no complain.

If I could read mind,
And never trusted the wrong ones, so blind.

27. IF I COULD GO BACK IN TIME

If I could go back in time,
Find the pride that should've been mine.

All those teen years I lived insecure,
The lost confidence was my cure.

'You're good enough' I would assure,
You're beautiful with heart so pure.

I would dress however I liked,
Whether my peers mocked me or called me wild.

I would let my hair down and let them flow,
Wouldn't try to cover up my inner glow.

I wouldn't let their words make me unsure,
Self-doubt and gaslighting I wouldn't endure.

Chubby or curvy, I wouldn't accept the body shame,
Those were all part of a dirty game.

Discern my strength from my introverted and reserved
nature,
Appreciate that extra mature and observant teenager.

If I could go back in time,
Find the pride that should've been mine.

I would thank my mentors in all forms,
Teacher, friends, family, all those who guided me
through storms.

I'll also find in my heart to forgive those who treated me
unfairly,
The ones who handed over my platter to the other
clearly.

Gratitude and forgiveness would set my little heart free,
Teen me would smile brighter and make friends more
confidently.

If I could go back in time,
Find the pride that should've been mine.

28. ADULTHOOD

You're an adult when you know you'll never be enough,
Perfection is a big bluff.

You're too white or you're too dark,
But who defined that perfect mark?

If you speak up, they call you smarty pants,
If you mind your business, they question your
intelligence.

You're too thin or you're too fat,
They just love to wear that judgy hat.

Glass skin and silky hair,
Is it even possible in this polluted air?

Talkative extrovert they call annoying,
Introverts appear excruciatingly boring.

The digits of your savings account always look scant,
There's no end to our greedy demands.

Generous sharing is called show off,
Stinginess gets snide scoff.

You're an adult when you know you'll never be enough,
Perfection is a big bluff.

It's about time we stop trying to fix that doesn't need to
be,
Accept our personalities and looks, freely.

Don't adult too hard that you lose your innocence,
That once was your true essence.

You're not brought into this world to please everybody,
Happier individual only can make a pleasant society.

Know that perfection is a relative concept,
There's no standard bar to accept.

You're an adult when you know you'll never be enough,
Perfection is a big bluff.

29. LIKE YOU?

Do I like you?
If you wonder, it's probably true.

If I'm awkward and make you uneasy,
It's probably because inside I'm feeling queasy.

If I'm cool and chill with you, there's no attraction,
If I'm acting dumb or cold, there's definitely affection.

Flirting skill, I never acquired,
Before my love life started, it retired.

If I can complement you, you're a bro,
If I can't do that or speak to you, there could be more.

Do I like you?
If you ponder, it's probably true.

Those cute ones might think I'm cold hearted,
They don't know my reactions around them get retarded.

Around others I'm courteous and friendly,
But with ones I fancy, I run away or appear angry.

How do I explain to them that I chicken out,
Too scared to even know what I might blurt out.

I can try to be a friend but clumsy,
Can't let my guard down and let you know my true
feelings openly.

If you saw those symptoms of my affliction,
For my hot cold behavior, I can only apologies for the
situation.

Do I like you?
If you have to ask, it's probably true.

30. WISH I WAS A BUTTERFLY

I wish I was a butterfly,
Gravity and rules I could defy.

No dangers to look out for, I could fly freely,
Be bolder and do whatever I want happily.

I would carry all the colors of life on my wings,
In the heavenly garden among nature, I would sing.

I could be a social butterfly with no judgement,
And fly high confident.

Be admired for my beauty, grace, and elegance,
Be a joy to be around for my wit and eloquence.

I wouldn't have to stay confined for safety,
I would be far away from problems of women's reality.

I wish I was a butterfly,
Gravity and rules I could defy.

I would be protected by nature until a cocoon,
Wouldn't let this harsh world have my innocence
consume.

As an adult I'll pull out my wings so strong,
Soar and dance in the sky where I belong.

I'll fly around rainbow to bring out the magic,
Be the cupid to all those romantic.

Though soft and fragile, I'll have a fierce flight,
Try to wound me and you'll forever lose me from your
sight.

Symbol of love, hope and bliss,
Reminder of beautiful life, you can't miss.

I wish I was a butterfly,
Gravity and rules I could defy.